Bible Study for Beginners

Based on

Seventy Years of Marginal Notes

Bernard Bull

Bible Study for Beginners Based on Seventy Years of Marginal Notes
ISBN: Softcover 979-8-89532-000-6
Copyright © 2024 by Bernard Bull

Parson's Porch Books is an imprint of Parson's Porch *&* Company (PP*&*C) in Cleveland, Tennessee. PP*&*C is a self-funded charity which earns money by publishing books of noted authors, representing all genres. Its face and voice is **David Russell Tullock** (dtullock@parsonsporch.com).

Parson's Porch *&* Company *turns books into bread & milk* by sharing its profits with the poor.

www.parsonsporch.com

Bible Study for Beginners

Acknowledgements

First my mother, Delma Bull, who had nine sons, of whom I was last. She lived and led a Christian life and directed my path.

God was gracious to save me when I was nine years old and provided teachers in church activities in my growing up years. I am grateful for every teacher and preacher who taught me.

Barbara Brown Bull, my wife of 60 plus years, who bought Bibles for me to study, and she was an example of the teaching therein. She also edited my writing.

Dr. Dean Haun, pastor of First Baptist Church, Morristown, Tennessee who is the best pastor/teacher a person could have. My writing reflects being under his teaching and preaching for the past five years. I have learned more from him than from most college and seminary professors. My Bible is marked with his insights which are many and deep and are reflected in these pages.

Contents

New Testament

Appendices

Seventy Years
of Bible Study Marginal Notes

When I was a baby my mother took me to the Cradle Roll Sunday School class at New Zion Baptist Church in McMinn County, Tennessee. At age five my family moved to Etowah, Tennessee where we joined First Baptist Church. At age nine I became a Christian by confessing my sin and asking Jesus to come into my life as my savior and LORD. I attended Sunday School, Church Training, participated in Bible Drill, Vacation Bible Schools, Royal Ambassadors and later worked as a leader in RAs.

At age 17 I prepared and delivered my first sermon in First Baptist Church of Delano, Tennessee.

During high school I carried a small print Bible to school to read during study hall. I wrote the date at the beginning of each chapter so I would know when I had read the entire Bible. I finished that Bible in 1959-60, my senior year. Since then I have read and marked in the Bible at least 13 times. During all those years, study also included daily devotionals and Sunday school. In the different translations of the Bible that I have read were numerous marginal notes and it is from those notes that this book is written.

It is my desire that these notes will assist people who are starting to study the Bible to get a quick start. These are totally my notes. There are no directly quoted passages, so you need to have your Bible beside you to read the text in question. This guide is NOT to be read cover to cover, but rather to use as you read and study the Bible.

When a reference is in parenthesis ( ) see the connection between the verses. Sometimes it is fulfillment of prophecy. Alphabetical list of Books and page numbers are in the appendix.

Your Notes Here

Old Testament

Genesis

1:2 God created… (Psalm 90:2)

3:6 The woman was lusting for the fruit because it looked good to eat. I believe she watched Satan eating it and he looked like he was enjoying it.

15:6 "Believed" is used for the first time in the Bible. It was counted to Abram as righteousness.

19:30-38 Incest. The two daughters of Lot had sex with their drunk father and produced two sons; Moab, father of the Moabites and Ben-Ammi, father of Ammonites. You cannot understand the Fall of Jericho without following their descendants. (Joshua 6:1-26)

22:2 God told Abraham to OFFER Isaac as a sacrifice. Notice the similarity of this event and the crucifixion of Jesus: wood-cross, Ram-lamb, blood sacrifice, substitute offering and both happened on Mt. Moriah. (Matt.27)

25:28 Isaac loved his son Esau but his wife, Rebekah loved Jacob. Parental favoritism is not a good thing.

26:34 The marriage of Esau to two Hittite women brought grief to Isaac and Rebekah.

34:3 The rape of Dinah, daughter of Jacob by Shechem, son of Hamor the Hivite resulted in all the men of their city being killed by the sword shortly after they were all circumcised.

35:19 Rachel was buried near Ephrath Bethlehem.

35: 21 The Tower of Eder is significant to the birth of Jesus in Luke chapter two.

35:22 Reuben had sex with Bilhah, his father's concubine.

49:4 Results of Reuben's behavior: Although he was the first born, he lost his "pre-eminence." You see in First Chronicles 5:1. Reuben lost his birthright.

Your Notes Here

Exodus

The people of Egypt gave gold and silver to the Israelites as they made their exit from Egypt. Ironically, they would later use the gold to make an idol.

Joseph and Mary received gold from the wise men, (and we do not know how many wise men) and they went down to Egypt. This fulfilled prophecy. (Hosea 11:1-4)

There is a summary of Israel leaving Egypt in Psalm 78. Psalm 105:37 states that no invalids were among Israelites leaving Egypt.

Exodus 19:4 God brought the Israelites out of Egypt "on eagle wings." See related note in Isaiah 40:31.

Exodus 20. The Ten Commandments are rarely shown correctly in today's world. The **two** stones were written on **both** sides as described in Exodus 32:15.

The Exodus of Israel from Egypt is summarized in a sermon by Paul in Acts 7:1-50.

Your Notes Here

Leviticus

1:3 Burnt offering must be a male without blemish.

3:17 This law is forever; eat no fat or blood.

5:1 If you are a witness and fail to speak up, it is a sin.

11:19 "Bat" is listed as a bird. Classification of animals by man did not take place until the 18th century. The identification on the "bat" as a "bird" has nothing to do with being an error in the Bible.

17:14 Do not eat the blood of any creature because life is in the blood.

18:19 No sex with a woman who is menstruating. Do not uncover her.

18:22 Homosexuality is absolutely forbidden. It is detestable.

19:26 No fortune telling or witchcraft.

20:11 Man must not have sex with his father's wife.

26:3-12 Being obedient to God brings blessings.

Your Notes Here

Numbers

1:2-15 Registration for the military outlined.

2:1 The 12 tribes were arranged in the shape of a cross, under their respective flags, with the tabernacle in the middle.

6:24-26 God told Moses to tell the priests (Aaron and sons) this prayer as a blessing on the Israelites.

11:31-32 Quail and other birds migrate between Africa and Europe. In Israel we saw Storks so numerous that it looked like a dark cloud.

13:30 Caleb was one of the 12 spies who went into the Promised Land. He encouraged the people with confidence that the people in the land could be conquered. The other positive spy was Joshua, who is also called Hoshea in 13:16.

24:9b Those who bless Israel will be blessed and those who curse Israel will be cursed. If you are a Christian, how can you bless Israel?

27:4 Women's Rights: Property was passed to the daughters because there was no son to receive the inheritance.

Your Notes Here

Deuteronomy

2:18 The land of the Ammonites was given to the descendants of Lot.

9:4b The people are being driven out because of their wickedness, not because of Israel's goodness.

13: Child sacrifice is detestable to God.

14:28 Who should eat from the food produced? The priest, the visitor, the fatherless, and the widow.

In each town where these people are fed the LORD will bless the work that is done.

22:5 There must be a difference between men's clothing and women's clothing. Cross dressing is detestable to the LORD. There is no unisex.

32:11 Eagles catch their young on his/her pinions.

Your Notes Here

Joshua

1:8 God told Joshua to think about the law all the time and to do what the law says and he would be successful and prosper.

6: Rahab, the harlot, was the only one in the city of Jericho with the foresight to see that God was on the side of the Israelites. The people of Jericho were descendants of Lot and his two sons who were born of his two daughters. These horrible people did such things as child sacrifice.

When the walls of Jericho fell it did NOT include the portion of the wall where Rahab and her family were housed. Her house was in the outer wall because she had let the spies down from her window.

7:22-26 Stupid Achan had taken war plunder that was prohibited: silver, a mantle and gold. To have these openly he would be immediately recognized. Why was his whole family stoned to death? By knowing and not telling, they were all guilty.

Your Notes Here

Judges

Overview of Judgment on Israel comes in these cycles:

Apostasy: falling away from God

Oppression: war with other tribes

Repentance: Seeing their error and turning back to God

Deliverance: God gives victory.

7: As God reduces the troops it is General Gideon, Major Gideon, Sergeant Gideon, Private Gideon, and then God gets the glory.

8: Gideon leads his people to defeat the Kings of Midian. The people wanted Gideon to become their king but he told them, the LORD will rule over you. The people donated all the gold from plunder and gave it to Gideon. He made an ephod, which became a thing to be worshipped. God, man, something; that is the degeneration of worship.

11: A military leader made a vow that upon returning home from victory, the first person to come out the front door of his house, he would burn to death as a sacrifice. It was his daughter!

12:6 The people of Ephraim when asked to say "Shibboleth" would say "siboleth." Because they could not pronounce the "sh" sound, they were identified as the enemy and 42,000 of them were killed.

Your Notes Here

Ruth

Ruth left her pagan country to follow her mother-in-law, Naomi and eventually married Boaz who was from Bethlehem. This marriage put Ruth in the family line to become the great grandmother of King David and therefore in the family line of Jesus. By following Naomi, Ruth chose her God as Yahwah. When she was gleaning in the fields of Boaz she was in the location where angels would appear to the shepherds at the birth of Jesus which was Ephrathah Bethlehem.

Your Notes Here

First Samuel

1:18-27 After Hannah prayed for a son and the Priest, Eli, said she would have a son, she put a smile on her face. She bore Samuel and when he was weaned, Hannah took him to Eli to live at the temple. The Bible says, "HE" worshipped there. Is the "HE" Samuel or Eli?

2:1-10 Longest prayer in the Old Testament by a woman.

2:11 and the boy ministered there before the LORD

3:7 Samuel did not yet know the LORD

Saul obeyed his father and went looking for their lost animals and there he met Samuel who anointed him to be the first king of Israel.

4: The Philistines did not die from touching the Ark of the Covenant but Israelites did die from touching it. Why? Unbelievers are not under the law but many did get sick in the presence of the Ark of the Covenant.

7:12 As a youth I sang, "here I raise my Ebenezer, ever by thy help… I had no idea what an Ebenezer was. It is a stone, marking a place. It is a monument.

11:7 This is an example of church and state.

13:8-10 State's overreach of the church.

15:12 Saul set up a monument to himself at Carmel and disobeyed the orders Samuel had given him from God. Rationalizing and lying does not alter the fact of disobedience.

15:24 Saul admits sin but blames it on "the people."

16:11-12 When Samuel sent for David, he said, they would NOT "sit down" until David arrived. When he did arrive, the LORD told them to "stand up." The term "sit down" meant they would not "close the circle of council." The same phrase is used in Jeremiah 23:22

31:11 The bodies of Saul and his three sons were cremated.

Your Notes Here

Second Samuel

11: Bathsheba was bathing after her menstruation and King David's dwelling, being the highest point in the city, was situated for looking down on the city. "Looking" may be the first step to adultery.

13: David's son Amnon acted sick to get his half-sister, Tamar, to care for him in his apartment. And there he raped her. What happened to Amnon? Tamar went to live with her brother, Absalom. Two years later Absalom had a party to which Amnon was invited.

13:28 After Amnon had a few drinks, Absalom orders his servants to kill Amnon. There are always consequences for sin.

16:21 Absalom had sex with David's concubines on the roof for all Israel to see. He was assuming power! Ahithopel who had suggested that Absalom have sex with the concubines committed suicide. 17:23

18:14-15 Absalom was killed by Joab and his armor-bearer after Absalom got his hair caught in tree and his mule ran on. There are consequences for sin!

20:3 The ten concubines of David were provided for in isolation until they died.

23:13 David was thirsty for water from the well in Bethlehem. Three of his men slipped through the Philistine lines and got the water and returned to King David.

23:16 David poured the water out as a drink offering to the LORD in gratitude for men risking their lives for him.

24:18 David built an altar on the thrashing floor of Araunah the Jebusite. This is the place where Abraham offered Isaac and it will be the place where King Solomon builds an altar at the dedication of the Temple. (First Kings 8:22) It is Mt.

Moriah. (First Chronicles 21:15 Araunah the Jebusite is called Ornan.)

Your Notes Here

First Kings

1:3 Abishag the Shunamite was brought in to keep King David warm in his old age. They were NOT intimate. She was identified as being beautiful.

8:5 At the celebration of the Temple there were so many animals to sacrifice that they could not be counted.

8:62 King Solomon had donated 22,000 cattle, and 120,000 sheep and goats.

11:3 Solomon had 700 wives and 300 concubines. In his older years, some of these women led him to worship false gods.

18: Elijah and the Priests of Baal were on Mt. Carmel. The Baal worshippers were cutting themselves and had tattoos. Israelites were prohibited from having tattoos . (Leviticus 19:28)

21:23 Here is a prophecy about the death of Jezebel.

(Second Kings 9:30 Jezebel is the first woman in the Bible to use make up. In 9:33-35 the prophecy is fulfilled exactly and Jezebel is dead, eaten by the dogs.)

22:21 Solomon's older halfbrother Adonijah asked if he could have Abishag the Shunamite for his wife. She was the beautiful woman who kept King David warm.

Because of this request, Solomon had Adonijah killed. This secured the kingship for Solomon.

Lesson: Be careful what you ask for!

Your Notes Here

Second Kings

4:42 A man brought 20 loaves of barley bread to Elisha but there were 100 men. Elisha told his servant to serve the bread. They ate and there was some left over.

(Matthew 14:13-21 and 15:20-39 Jesus feeding the 5,000 and the 4,000)

5:23-26 Greedy Gehazi lied to Elisha and got leprosy. Naman had just been healed of leprosy by dipping in the Jordan River as instructed by Elisha.

Lesson: Do not lie to a man of God, or anyone else.

9:30 Jezebel painted her eyes and fixed her hair. This is the first mention in the Bible of a woman using makeup. Painted eyes are also mentioned in Jeremiah 4:30 and in Ezekiel 23:40.

13:21 The man who was being put in the tomb and hurriedly dropped on the bones of Elisha was "revived." This is not a man coming back from the dead but a man getting his breath back.

15:19 When Assyria invaded Israel, the wealthy men were taxed 50 shekels of silver.

18:4 Hezekiah destroyed things of false worship, including the bronze snake that Moses made because people were burning incense to it. (Numbers 21:6-9)

Your Notes Here

First Chronicles

1:19 The son of Eber was Peleg, whose name means "division." It was in his time that the earth was divided.

2:15 The youngest son of Jesse was David but most emphasis in that culture was placed on the oldest.

4:9 Prayer of Jabez, when he asked God to enlarge his territory.

10:13 Saul was disobedient to God and even used a medium's services. He lost his kingdom and his life.

11:19 David refused to drink the water that his men brought from the well in Bethlehem.

12: 2 The kinsmen of Saul were ambidextrous and they joined forces with David. They could shoot bows and sling rocks with both left and right hands.

29:3-7 Ideas for fund raising: King David gave some of his wealth of gold and silver for the building of the temple and his followers then gave gold, silver, bronze and iron.

Leadership starts at the top.

Your Notes Here

Second Chronicles

1:11 Solomon asked for wisdom to govern. Wisdom is from God and is different from human knowledge. (Psalm 111:10)

3:1 The Temple was built on Mt. Moriah, the place of two former events; Abraham's offering of Isaac and David's altar of repentance; and a future event of Jesus being beaten before the crucifixion. (John 19:1)

7:14 God's promise to King Solomon at the completion of the Temple at Jerusalem was that the way out of catastrophe was humility, prayer and repentance. It was true then and it is true now.

16:13 A cremation of Asa took place. (Jeremiah 34:5 tells of the cremation of Zedekiah, King of Judah)

20:1 Jehoshaphat (Jehovah Judges) got the country following God's law and three groups, Moabites, Ammonites and other Ammonites came against Jehoshaphat.

Lesson: Satan spends minimum time on marginal Christians and major time on mature Christians.

26:16-18 Here is an example of the state interfering with the church. As a result, King Uzziah became a leper for life.

28:12-15 Compare the results here to the story Jesus told about the man on the road to Jericho. (Luke 10:25-37)

32:6-8 Courage and leadership: Hezekiah told the people of his army to not fear the enemy which was flesh against the God of Judah. This gave the people confidence.

Your Notes Here

Ezra

2:61 A man took the family name of the wife. Very unusual.

7:8 Ezra's group walked four months to get to Jerusalem from Babylon.

7:24 No tax on people who worked in the church.

8:21 Ezra, a priest, would not ask the King for military escort to Jerusalem because he had clearly expressed his belief in God's protection.

8:31 Ezra arrived safely in Jerusalem to begin rebuilding the walls of the city. Nehemiah (2:9) on the other hand was a civil servant and not a priest. The King gave him a military escort.

Your Notes Here

Nehemiah
(cup bearer to the King)

2:1 Nehemiah was talking to King Artaxerxes and the King asked him what he wanted. Between the questions and the answer Nehemiah PRAYED. He requested permission to return to Jerusalem to rebuild the wall around the city.

2:9 The King sent a military escort to protect Nehemiah's caravan of supplies. (Ezra 8:21) did not ask for escort.

4:9 Building the wall: they prayed and stationed guards.

8:2-8 Ezra got out the parchment, the Law of Moses (the Torah) and read it aloud to the people from early morning until noon. The people could see Ezra up on the platform and when he opened the book, they all stood up. This is probably why congregations stand today for the reading of scripture. The people held up their hands and bowed to the ground in praise of God. Then 12 Levites read and gave instructions to groups of people to be sure they understood the teaching. This was a tutorial similar to present day Sunday School.

9:1-10 Nehemiah tells the story of Israel's repentance and recommitment.

Your Notes Here

Esther
In Persia, now called Iran

1:16 If the Queen disobeys the King, all the women will misbehave toward their husbands.

1:22 Thus the King sent a letter to every region, in their own language, every man is lord of his own house.

A man's home is his castle.

4:15 This may be the time for which you came into the kingdom. This is what Mordecai told Esther.

4:16 Esther requested her people to fast and pray for three days. If a person went to the King without being summonsed, he/she could be executed. Esther was willing to risk death to save her people.

7:10 Haman was executed on the gallows he had built for killing Mordecai.

9:10 And Haman's 10 sons were killed.

10:31 Purim-fasting and prayer were established in Jewish custom as a celebrations of these events.

Your Notes Here

Job

1:18-20 When Job heard the news of the death of his children he tore his clothing and shaved his head and then he worshipped. Tearing clothing in grief goes back to Genesis 37:29 when Reuben was grieved because he thought his brother Joseph was dead.

2:10 Job tells his wife not to expect just good things from God and not trouble. Be faithful in good times and bad times. He is the God of the mountain and the valley.

2:13 The gift of "being there." Power of presence.

19:23-26 Job wished to make a permanent record that God the Redeemer lives and even if dry skin is destroyed, still in his flesh, he will see God.

28:28 Wisdom is to respect the LORD, which should lead you to depart from evil.

34:14-15 If God withdrew his spirit and breath, all people would become dust. (Gen. 3:19, Ecc.3:20)

God blessed Job with twice as much as he had before.

Your Notes Here

The Psalms

8:2 Praise God from infants and children. (Matt. 21:16)

19:14 May my words and thoughts be pleasing to my LORD and redeemer.

22:1&16-18 Words that Jesus spoke from the cross. (Matt. 28:46)

22:31 Note that this Psalm ends with great victory.

34:20 No bone in the body of Jesus will be broken.

46: This Psalm was the inspiration for Martin Luther's great hymn, A Mighty Fortress is Our God.

51: David's confession after his adultery with Bathsheba.

53:1 April Fool's Day. To say there is no God.

66: This is a hymn. 8-10 is community thanksgiving, 11-20 is an individual's thanksgiving.

69:22...gave vinegar...Jesus on the cross. (Matt. 27:34)

84:10 I would rather be a custodian in the house of God than to be a bartender in a casino.

89:9 God rules the surging sea. Jesus calms the Sea of Galilee. (Luke 8:24-25)

111:10 Wisdom is begun by reverence for the LORD.

118:22 Masons were making rectangular blocks and one broke into two triangles. It was thrown aside, later to become the capstone. In Matt. 21:42 Jesus mentioned this. Jesus is the chief corner stone.

119:11 Memorize God's word to avoid sin. This Psalm is based on the Hebrew alphabet.

146:8 God curing the blind. (Matt. 9:27-30

Your Notes Here

Proverbs

There are 31 chapters in Proverbs. If you read the chapter corresponding to the day of the month, you can read the book in one month. For several years I read it aloud every month. It has great practical value.

1:7 Wisdom begins with reverence for God.

6:16-19 Seven things God hates: These have to do with eyes, tongue, hands, heart, feet, false witness, and people who sow seeds of discord among relatives.

These character traits are evident in Haman in the book of Esther and the life of Samson in Judges.

6:30 A starving man may have excuses for stealing food, but if caught he must pay back seven times as much.

10:1 Death will not come to a good man by starving. The LORD will not let it happen.

13:8 A poor man does not worry about being held for ransom.

14:31 If you mistreat poor people you are disrespecting the God who made them.

15:1 Avoid anger by speaking softly.

17:22 Being happy does a body good, like good medicine.

17:28 A silent fool may be seen as wise. A quiet person is seen as intelligent.

22:1 Silver and gold: not to be chosen over a good name.

23:13 Do not fail to discipline a child. A corrective spanking will not kill him/her.

25:6-7 Do not take a seat of honor or place of honor. It is better to be called up than put down. (Luke 14:7-11)

25:20 Do not be jolly around a heavy heart because that is like putting Alka-Seltzer in a soft drink.

26:11 Repeating a mistake is like a dog eating its own vomit.

26:18-19 If you deceive someone and say, "It was only a joke," it is like throwing a fire bomb or shooting them with an arrow.

27:7 The bird that leaves the nest and the man who strays from home need to beware of the cat.

27:14 Loud morning people blessing others will be taken as a curse.

29:15 It is better to spank a child than to leave him/her to make decisions alone. This will bring shame to the parents. Children need boundaries.

31: This chapter should be read to honor NOBLE women.

Women who respect God are to be praised.

Your Notes Here

Ecclesiastes

3: There is a time for....

5:12 Work can help you sleep, but material things keep a rich man awake.

7:1 Being respected is like good medicine.

7:5 Rebuke from a wise man is better than praise from a fool.

10:2 If you are wise, your thoughts lead you to the right, but a fool is lead to the left.

10:10 Sharpen your ax or work harder at cutting.

Your Notes Here

The Song of Solomon

2:7; 3:5; 7:10 This man and woman love each other when it is appropriate.

2:16 Proper sleeping position. Man's left arm under her head so he can embrace her with his right hand.

4:16 and 7:13 The wonderful fragrance of mandrakes. Every flavor of the fragrance is stored up for the lover.

(Gen 30:14) Reuben got mandrakes for Leah, his mother.

6:13 Shulamite: The young lady who kept King David warm in his old age, and David's son was killed for wanting her as a wife. King Solomon ordered his death.

7:9 Describing a "French Kiss."

7:13 Mandrakes mentioned again.

Your Notes Here

Isaiah

Concerning Judah and Jerusalem

1:18 Your red sin can become white as snow. (Psalm 51:7 and Rev. 7:14)

2:4 Weapons of war will be dismantled and turned into agricultural implements.

7:14; 9:6-7 Prophecy about the birth of Jesus 700 years before he was born.

11:3-4 Jews believed that a true prophet could judge without his eyes or ears. By implication the prophet could judge by smell. Consider this in the crucifixion of Jesus when he was blindfolded. (Mark 14:65; Luke 22:63) When Jesus was slapped and the Jewish leaders and their guards ask him to prophecy which one hit him.

24:5 When mankind forsakes the law of God the earth will be polluted.

26:3 If you keep your mind on God, you will be at peace.

28:16 God said He was putting a precious cornerstone, a foundations stone, in Zion. (Jesus in Eph.2:19-21)

35:5-6 Blind people will be able to see and deaf will hear, the lame will walk and the dumb will speak. All these were fulfilled by Jesus. (Luke 7:22)

40:8 God's word is forever, it will not fade.

40:31 Those who pursue God will be strengthened.

What is being described by: **flying** eagle, **running**, **walking**? In Israel a Jewish man explained to me his interpretation of this verse. "God led the children of Israel out of Egypt with the speed of a flying eagle. They ran to fight the battles in claiming the land. They walked in peace the Promised Land."

My interpretation is that God raises us up, **Salvation**, *flying* free from the penalty of sin. We *run* in life's race with **Sanctification**, freeing us from the power of sin; and we will *walk* with Him in **Glorification**, freed from the presence of sin.

53: Must read the entire chapter and see it as a prediction about the crucifixion of Jesus has born our grief, sorrow, wounded, etc.

56:7b Jesus quoted this verse in "cleansing the temple."

(Matt. 21:13; Mark 11:17; Luke 19:45)

49:6 A light for the Gentiles. (Luke 2:32)

61:1-3 These passages are quoted in Luke 2:18-19, except the second part of verse 2, because the Day of Vengeance is still to come.

65: Most often misquoted: You see it in drama, art and hear it in music and it sounds so good together: The Lion and the Lamb. But the correct scripture is "wolf and lamb."

Your Notes Here

Jeremiah

1:5 God knew Jeremiah before he was a fetus. Call called Jeremiah and set him apart.

3:6 God said Israel had gone under every green tree and committed adultery. Idolatry! (Compare this passage to

John 1:48 Nathan under a fig tree.)

17:13 Those who forsake God will have their names written in the dirt. Was that what Jesus was doing in the story of the "woman taken in adultery.'? (John 8:6) This is said to be the only thing that Jesus wrote on earth.

Your Notes Here

Lamentations

Sometimes called the Lamentations of Jeremiah.

2: God's judgment on the city.

3: Hope of relief comes because of God's loving kindness.

3:22-24 The only reason we are not consumed is because of God's love which is new every morning.

3: 37-39 Good and bad comes from God. Compare this to what Job said. (Job 2:10)

4: Sorrow of the people because of the siege.

5: Prayer for mercy and deliverance.

Your Notes Here

Ezekiel

4:14-15 Using dried human excrement for fuel was distasteful to Ezekiel so he asked God to allow him to use dried cow manure instead. God allowed it in His permissive will.

18:6 Here is a warning to not have sexual intercourse when the female is menstruating and not to commit adultery.

23:40 Painted eyes and jewelry in order to be attractive to men for whom they had sent. (2 Kings 9:30 Jezebel)

33:11 It is the desire of God that wicked people would turn back to Him. He does not desire death for the wicked but repentance.

Your Notes Here

Daniel

Facing Trials and Temptations

Set convictions early, make a courteous stand, suggest alternatives, suffer consequences, and be willing to die for your convictions. (Dr. Dean Haun)

1: Four enslaved Jewish youth on a vegetarian diet looked better than all the other youth on the King's food and they were wiser.

1:7 Daniel was named Belteshazzar; Hananiah was named Shadrach; Mishel was named Meshach; and Azariah was named Abednego. All the new names were for false gods.

3: After refusing to worship the gold image the three, other than Daniel, were thrown into the fiery furnace. Serve God regardless of the circumstances. These three men were promoted to places of leadership in the government.

4:29 For all he had built, the King claimed he had done it by his own mighty power and majestic glory. He then lost his mind. Those characteristic belong to God alone and cannot be claimed by a human.

4:34 As the King returned to God he regained his sanity.

6:16-24 Because Daniel prayed to the God of Judah he was put in a den of lions. But God delivered him safely and the men who accused Daniel, along with their entire families were cast into the lion's den and immediately eaten. Remember the whole family of Achan was killed recorded in Joshua 7:24-26; 22:20; and I Chron 2:7.

The prophecy of Daniel concerning the Second Coming of Christ needs extensive study.

Your Notes Here

Hosea

The prophet is told to marry a prostitute. This is an illustration of how Israel had been unfaithful to God by worshipping idols.

2:13 Here is another example of a woman dressing in jewels to attract lover.

3: God's love is constant and He wants the sinner to return to Him. This is illustrated by Hosea purchasing his wife back to himself. The Israelites will return to God and His blessings in the last days.

11:1 and 13:4 Prophecy that Messiah, Jesus, will come out of Egypt. (Matthew 2:15)

14: Return to God in repentance and forgiveness for all your sins.

14:9 There are two choices: The upright follow God and the unrighteous fall.

The rain that falls on a dead tree makes it rot.

The rain that falls on a live tree helps it grow.

You can be made alive in Christ Jesus.

Your Notes Here

Joel

1:5 and 3:3 Sins mentioned in this book are: drunkards, human trafficking boys for prostitution and girls for wine.

1:14 Call to assemble at God's house and repent.

2:13 There is an ancient custom of ripping clothing when in distress. God wants our grief to come from the heart and for us to return to him.

2:32 To be saved, call on the name of the LORD.

3:10 Prepare for war. Turn your farm implements into weapons of war.

Your Notes Here

Amos

2:7 A man and his son having sexual intercourse with the same woman is a disgrace to God.

3:8 and 11 Prophecy of coming destruction, similar to that of the plagues in Egypt and Sodom and Gomorrah.

4: Some will be taken away with fishhooks in their skin. With all that punishment the people would not repent.

8:11 The day is coming when God will not be heard. There were 400 years of silence between the Old and New Testaments.

9:15 Israel will never be forced out of their land. God's promise!

Your Notes Here

Obadiah

Obadiah proclaims that Edom, the descendants of Esau, will fall. The feud continues between them and the descendants of Jacob, but Jacob's will prevail. The Edomites were not all they thought they were and they disregarded God.

Your Notes Here

Jonah

The word "whale" does not appear in this book!

1:17 A great fish swallowed Jonah and he was there for three days and nights. This event was referenced by Jesus in Matthew 12:38-42 where He talks of being in the grave for three days and nights.

2:1 In the belly of the great fish, Jonah prayed to God.

3:6-8 A decree from the King was announced that everyone must fast and they individually must repent.

3: Jonah preached and the people of Ninevah repented.

The book of Jonah shows the great mercy that God has for people.

Your Notes Here

Micah

4:3 Hope for the last days. Implements of war will be reshaped as farm equipment.

4:8 Migdol Eder: watchtower…to you they will come.

(Genesis 48:7)

5:2-5 Prophesy concerning Jesus who would be born in a specific place: Bethlehem Ephrathah in Judah. He will be the Prince of Peace.

You cannot understand the story of the birth of Jesus, Christmas, in the New Testament without these passages in Micah. Jesus will be born at the watchtower near where Rachel was buried.

6:8 Seek justice, mercy and walk humbly with God.

Your Notes Here

Nahum

1:1-3 There is a saying, "The wheel of justice grinds slowly but exceedingly fine." It may seem like punishment does not come soon enough to evil doers.

God is not easily angered but punishment will come in due time.

3:19 When evil people fall there will be rejoicing.

Your Notes Here

Habakkuk

The writer complains and God answers

1:3-4 This reads like today's new reports.

2:4b This verse is quoted in Romans 1:17.

2:15 Getting someone drunk and beating him down in order to see his nakedness and shame. (Noah's son)

3:17-19 Habakkuk declares that regardless of the circumstances, no matter how bad, he will maintain his joy in knowing the LORD. Without vegetables or meat to eat, he will still trust the LORD, who is his strength.

That would be my prayer as well.

Your Notes Here

Zephaniah

Warning of destruction and redemption

1:9 Superstition about stepping on the threshold of a house is declared here. In First Samuel 5:5 the false god Dagan had fallen on its face on the threshold of the temple because it had been beside the Ark of the Covenant. To step over the threshold was what pagans do.

3:17 What a joyful thought! God is rejoicing over you.

Your Notes Here

Haggai

Dedicated to rebuilding the temple in Jerusalem.

1:1 and 14 This prophecy took 24 days.

1:3 God's house should be as good or better than the houses of the members of the congregation.

1:7 Get started!

Your Notes Here

55

Zechariah

Call for national repentance

4:6 Victory will come for the few and weak because it will be done by God's Spirit.

7:10 Do nothing to harm: widows, orphans, the poor or immigrants.

9:9b The victorious, humble King comes riding on a donkey's colt. (Matthew 21:5 and John 12:15)

11:12-13 Thirty pieces of silver which were thrown to the potter. (Matthew 27:9-10;)

Price paid if a bull gores a slave. (Exodus 21:32)

Price paid to Judas to betray Jesus. (Matt. 26:15)

12:10 The one they pierced. (John 19:34,37; Rev. 1:7)

12:14 Even today the men and women have a separate place to pray at the Western Wall in Jerusalem.

Your Notes Here

Malachi

1:11 God is to be praised all day and in every nation.

2:15 Man is to be faithful to his wife.

2:16 Divorce was not in God's intention. One man for one woman for life. (Deu. 24:1; Matt. 5:31-31; Matt. 19:4-9)

3:1 Prophecy concerning the coming of John the Baptist. (Matt. 3:3, 11:10)

3:8 Giving a title (10%) and extra offerings is expected of God's people. If not given, you are robbing God.

   (Malachi 3:8-12)

3:10 The tithes and offerings are to be brought to God's house. (2 Kings 7:2)

4:5 Watch for the coming of Elijah.

(Matt. 11:1 and Luke 1:17)

Your Notes Here

Matthew

The only gospel writer to use the word "church."

2:5 Prophecy fulfilled. (Micah 5:2) Bethlehem

2:9 The Magi did NOT come to the birthplace of Jesus. When they arrive the family was in a house.

The Magi, and we do not know how many, were led by a star. The Children of Israel were led by a cloud by day and a fire by night. (Ex. 13:20-22) The Magi brought gold for the King, incense for a Priest, and myrrh for His burial.

3:2 Individuals will receive the Holy Spirit or fire.

7:1-5 Most often misquoted or incorrectly interpreted. This paragraph is about being fair and just. (Lev. 19:15)

Use the same yardstick for yourself that you use for others. (I Cor. 5:12) How to judge **in** the church.

9:4 (Mark 2:9, Luke 5:22) Which is easier to say?

A. Forgiveness is invisible B. walking is visible, which is provable or disprovable. A is easier to say. Therefore if you can do the hard one, it is understood you can do the easy one. If a swimmer dives from the 20 foot board would someone then say, "Yes, but can you dive from the 2 foot board?" That is a given. Jesus can forgive sin!
8:34 The pigs were gone into the sea. The herdsmen and townspeople put commerce before Christ.
12:39 Jesus refers to Jonah.
12:43 Evil spirits do not like water. The possessed pigs ran into the Sea of Galilee. (Mark 5:13)
14:13 Where was this "solitary place?" It was out in the sea of Galilee.
16:1 Red at night, sailors' delight, red in the morning, sailors take warning. That popular poem is based on this scripture. What are the signs of the times?

19:18 Jesus asked the Rich Young Ruler about keeping the commandments, but He only mentioned the bottom six, not the top four related to God. The rich man showed no dependence on God.

20:1-16 Jesus reminded the Chief Priest what the Old Testament teaches. (Psalm 8:2; Habakkuk 3:17-19) Praise from infants and children, God ordained.

25:14 Each man received according to his ability. Each could have been successful but the bad servant had an attitude of ingratitude.

26: In Peter's denial of Jesus, he was recognized twice by females. The first was a slave girl, then another recognized his dialect. Why was he recognized by females? Just curious.

27:46 Quoted from (Psalm 22:1)

28:11 Would Roman soldiers report to a Jewish priest? Would Roman soldiers lie to the public for the Jewish leaders? I think NOT. (Mark 14:43- 53)

28:19-20 Jesus gives directions to His disciples to go and teach others how to become disciples.

Your Notes Here

Mark

2:9 (Matt. 9:5)

3:22 "down from Jerusalem" was going north.

4:25 How can you "take away" what someone does not have? Consider bonus questions on a test at school. The intelligent students get it right and raise the average grade which lowers the average for weaker students. The grades 100, 70, 65, average 78.3 but 105, 70, 65, average 80. A student with a grade of 65 in the first case is 13.3 down but in the second case the student is 15 points down.

5:19-20 The demon possessed man that Jesus healed wanted to go with Jesus but was told to go home and tell others what God had done for him. But he told everyone what JESUS had done for him. He recognized the Divinity of Jesus.

10:13-14 (Matt. 19:13-15, Luke 18:15-17) Only Mark uses the term "indignant."

14:44 In the Garden of Gethsemane Jesus was under the control of Jewish guards, not Roman soldiers.

14:53 Peter was warming by the fire with the guards.

14:65 (Matt.16:21) They blindfolded Jesus and hit him, then asked Him to identify who had hit him. Based on (Isaiah 11:2-4) should be able to smell.

Your Notes Here

Luke

The only Gentile writer of the Gospels.

1:79 The term "Shadow of death" is also in

(Isaiah 9:2, Matt. 4:16b)

2: The birth of Jesus

The priestly shepherds caught the baby sheep in swaddling cloth and protected them until they were taken to Jerusalem for sacrifice. The sheep had to be perfect without blemish. The shepherds knew exactly where the Watchtower was and RAN to where Jesus was born.

2:28 Simeon and 2:36 Anna. With all the boy babies coming to be circumcised or just babies with their parents, these two people, Simeon and Anna, knew exactly who Jesus was.

4:16-20 Jesus stood to read scripture and sat down to teach.

8:2-3 Well-to-do women gave money to the ministry of Jesus and His disciples.

12:3 Warning for FACEBOOK users.

9:9 Herod wants to see Jesus after John's beheading.

13:31 Jesus is warned that Herod wants to kill Him.

23:8 Herod wants to see Jesus do a miracle.

16:19-31 The rich man and Lazarus. This story ends with the rich man in hell and wanting someone to tell his brothers to repent. But if people will not believe

the law and the prophets (OT) they will not believe even if someone were to raise from the dead. This is exactly what Jesus did and some still will not believe.

17:11-17 Ten men with leprosy were told by Jesus to see the priest. On the way they were CLEANSED. But one man, a Gentile, returned to thank Jesus who is the Great High Priest, and this man was WELL.

19:9 Zacchaeus, the tax collector repented and received salvation. The Rich Young Ruler went always sorrowful because of his possessions.

Do not let your "stuff" keep you from the Savior.

Your Notes Here

John

1:1 Jesus, the Word, was God before the beginning.

1:7Grace without truth is liberalism.

Truth without grace is legalism.

Receive the grace of Jesus and live by his truth. A good example is (John 8:4,11) woman taken in adultery below.

2:1-10 water into wine…For your party: "Invite Jesus, obey what he says, serve for Him and give God the glory." (Charles Fowler, devotional for Disaster Relief.)

3:16 The gospel in one verse.

4:28-29 The disciples went to a Samarian town, a woman came to the well and talked to Jesus. The disciples brought no one back but the woman brought the whole town.

5:8 A lame man was healed.

5:14 Jesus sees the man again and tells him to stop sinning. This shows the compassion and constraint of Jesus. Grace and truth.

5:48 Jesus claims that Moses wrote about Him. (Deut. 18:15-19) Christ claimed to be divine.

8:4 The woman taken in adultery was accused by Pharisees who misquoted (Lev. 20:20-10; Deu. 22:22) Both the man and the woman must die but they brought only the woman. What did Jesus write in the dirt? Maybe he wrote the names of the men and the wind blew the names away. The Pharisees would have been familiar with this verse (Jeremiah 17:13)

8:59 The Temple refers to the Temple compound, which included the court of the women, court of Gentiles etc. Jesus was never recorded to be inside the temple. When Joseph and Mary went to get Jesus, it was Mary who questioned him and women were not allowed in the temple, only in the court of the women. (Luke 2:48)

11:16 The one often called "Doubting Thomas", in this verse he declares himself willing to die with Jesus.

13:4 A great example of servant leadership when Jesus washed the feet of his followers.

14:1-6 A favorite passage for funerals because Christians have a future of joy in a home in heaven.

20:6-7 The folded cloth at the table signaled to the wait staff that the diner will return. Jesus is coming back.

21:9 It is said that this charcoal fire is the same as the fire where Peter warmed himself when Jesus was arrested.

Your Notes Here

Acts

4:1 Peter and John were arrested by the temple guard and by the Sadducees, who did not believe in the resurrection of the dead. A belief in the resurrection of the dead was being taught by Peter and John concerning Jesus.

5:1 Ananias and his wife Sapphira tried to cheat God by withholding funds from the church and lying about it. Both of them died and were buried that day.

7:1-53 Stephen gives a summary of the Old Testament.

6:1-5 Note the selected men have Greek names. They were to be sure their widows were not neglected.

10:8-20 Peter sees a vision of "clean" and "unclean". He concludes that Gentiles are not unclean. He shows this by going into the home of Cornelius, who was a Gentile.

10:34 Jesus is for every nationality. Nothing in this event is about diet. The dream is an analogy about people groups.

10:18 In many parts of the world it is considered rude to KNOCK. To "call out" is good. (Rev 3:20) If there is a "knock" who would "hear my voice?"

12:13 Peter "knocked" at the center entrance and Rhoda recognized his voice.

19:9 Paul first taught in the synagogue for three months but then he and the disciples taught in a school (Hall of Tyrannus) for two years.

20:7-10 This is the first time "Sunday" is used. Paul preached for a long time. Eutychus" fell from the third floor and the people said he was dead but Paul declared the he was NOT dead. (See appendix, 'Raising the Dead ')

23:16-22 The young boy, the nephew of Paul, heard men scheming to kill Paul. He told the authorities and saved Paul's life. The commander "held his hand," indicating that he was a child. He is a nameless hero in the Bible.

26:23 Jesus would be first raised from the dead!

(1 Cor. 15:20) Christ was "first fruits", "primary" unlike Lazarus (John 11:14) Jesus did not have to die again

Your Notes Here

Romans

1:27 Homosexuality is a perversion (Lev 18:22, 20:13)

3:23 all have sinned

5:8 In our sinful condition, Christ died for us.

8:28 For all who love God, He works out everything for good.

10:9-10 To be saved a person must believe that Jesus is LORD and confess that God raised Him from the dead.

12:2 Do not be like the world, use your mind to follow God's will. The theological word for growing in Christ is Sanctification.

16:1-2 Paul asked the church members to welcome Phoebe because she was a servant at the church in Cenchrea.

Your Notes Here

First Corinthians

1:17 Paul came to preach the gospel, not to give water baptism.

5:9-11 Judging people within the church is the responsibility of the church. Paul advised members to not associate with immoral people- not even to eat with them. (Eph. 5:11 expose deeds of darkness.)

6:9-11 After a list of immoral behaviors Paul said some of the members WERE, past tense, had been, immoral but they changed and became followers of Jesus.

7:5 Husbands and wives have two reasons to not have sexual intercourse: when they are having a time of prayer, worship and when the woman is having her

menstruation. (Lev. 15:19&24)

10:13 Testing only goes as far as a person can bear. God will protect you.

12:15-20 Do not negate your own influence. Do not think less of yourself or others than you ought. Do not think more of yourself than you ought.

15:20 The resurrection of Jesus is primary.

16:9&13 Where there is opportunity, there will be opposition. Be alert and be brave in Christ.

Your Notes Here

Ephesians

"In Christ' is used 37 times in this book.

1:3 & 13 Father, Son and Holy Spirit

2:8 God's gift, by His grace, is that we are saved by faith.

5:1 If we are "in Christ" we do not do things improper for God's people. He specifically mentions greed, impurity, and sexual immorality.

5:11 Christians should expose the deeds of darkness because Christians are "children of light."

5:19 Music for the LORD comes from the heart.

5:31 Husband and wife are one flesh. (Gen. 2:24)

6:1 Children, love your parents in the LORD. (Ex, 20:12)

Your Notes Here

Philippians

2:10-11 Every knee will bow at the name of Jesus. (Romans 14:11; Isa. 45:23b

4:13-14 Do not gaze back; press on toward heaven in Christ Jesus. (Lot's wife, Gen. 19:26)

Your Notes Here

Colossians

2:8 The only use of the word "philosophy" in the Bible is here and it is a warning to beware of human traditions.

2:9 Declaration of the deity and humanity of Jesus.

3:18-25 How to have peace in the home.

4:2-5 Keep praying.

Your Notes Here

First Thessalonians

Paul uses the word "brethren" 21 times and "grace" over 100 times.

1:2 The three words from (1 Cor. 13) used here: faith, hope, love.

2:9 Paul was what we call today, bi-vocational preachers because he was a tent maker.

4:3 Do not have "fornication," any form of illicit sex.

4:16-17 Process of ascension into heaven when Christ returns.

5:2 When will Christ return?

Your Notes Here

Second Thessalonians

3:7 Paul worked so he would not be a burden on anyone.

3:10 If able bodied people do not work they should not eat. Although we are waiting for the coming of Christ, we should keep working to provide for ourselves.

3:13 Do not get tired of doing good.

Your Notes Here

First Timothy

2:1 We should pray for governmental officials that they will govern in such a way that we can live a quiet life in peace and in holiness.

2:9 Christian women should be attractive in godliness and not in sexy clothing and jewelry.

4:13 Public reading of scripture, especially when few people had access to printed scripture.

5:8 If a person does not provide for his family he is worse than an unbeliever.

6:10 Often misquoted as, "The love of money is the root of all evil." That is not true. Sins like rape, incest, etc. do not involve money. Correctly it says, "The love of money is the root of ALL KINDS of EVIL."

Your Notes Here

Second Timothy

1:5 The value of a Godly mother and grandmother.

2:5 Athletes cannot be winners without following the rules.

2:17 Correct people who depart from God's truth.

3:12 Following Christ will bring persecution.

3:15 Timothy, like most Jewish boys, had been studying scripture "since infancy."

3:16 All of God's inspired word is useful for preparing one to do good works. His word is for teaching, reproof, and correcting.

4:2 Preaching should be year round for three reasons: correction, rebuke, and encouragement.

4:8 How does one get the "crown of righteousness?"

Keep the faith to the end of the race. The saved sinner will be DECLARED righteous by Christ.

Your Notes Here

Titus

1:5-9 Characteristics of church leaders

3:10 A person bringing division into the church should be warned twice. If not corrected he/she should be avoided.

3:14 Do productive, honorable work.

Your Notes Here

Philemon

1:2 Most church groups of the day met in homes.
1:8 Paul appealed to Christian friends to receive a man who became a Christian while Paul was in prison, although the man, Onesimus, was a runaway slave.

Your Notes Here

Hebrews

My title is "Growing to Glorification"
Jesus is absolutely supreme.
1:4&14 Jesus is superior to angels.
2:11 Jesus calls Christians, brothers. (Matt.28:10)
2:15 If you are afraid of death you are in a lifetime of bondage. Jesus defeated death for you.
3:3 Jesus is superior to Moses
4:12-13 Nothing is hidden from God. He even sees our thoughts and attitudes.
4:16 We may approach his throne boldly.
7:25 Come to God through Jesus.
9:22 There must be shedding of blood for forgiveness.
9:27 Once to die and then the judgment. People do not die in the hospital and then come back to life.
11: Roll call of the faithful. These are all from the Hebrew scripture because the New Testament was not completed at that time.
11:16 Christians are "looking for the city that God prepared. (13:14)
13:4 Sex within marriage must be undefiled. God will judge the sexually immoral and adulterers.
13:14 This is not home! Christians are still looking for the eternal city.

Your Notes Here

James (Jacob)

1:2 Christians will face trials.

1:13 God does not tempt people.

1:27 We have to take responsibility for widows and orphans.

2:14 If you have "faith" (a verb) you do something because of it. Feed the hungry, care for the sick etc.

2:25 Rahab is recognized by her deed. (Josh.2:4; Hebrews 11:31)

3:9 The tongue can be for good or bad.

4:15 Saying "I will____" is dangerous because we do not know what the future holds. Christians should say, "I will, if the LORD wills it."

5:1-6 Warning to rich people.

5:7-20 Promises for brothers in Christ.

Your Notes Here

First Peter

2:6-8 Unbelievers trip and fall over the living Corner stone, which is Jesus. (Isa. 8:14)
2:24 By His stripes we are healed. (Isa.53:5)
3:15 If someone asks you why you are a Christian, you should be able to tell him/her.

Your Notes Here

Second Peter

1:4-7 God's divine power allows Christians to participate in His nature and add to our faith, goodness, knowledge, self-control, perseverance, godliness, brotherly kindness, and love. The big word for this is Sanctification.

1:21 The Bible is the written word of God.

2:22 A cleaned up pig will return to the mud. (Proverbs 26:11)

3:13 A new world is coming where there is only goodness. The earth was destroyed by water but the next time it will be destroyed by fire.

Your Notes Here

First John

1:1-7 If we have fellowship with God we will have fellowship with fellow believer. If we do not, we are walking in darkness.
1:9 God forgives our sins when we confess them.
3:9 Christians cannot practice sinning but righteousness.
4:2 Jesus is God in human flesh.
4:4 Christ in you is greater than the one in the world.
  (Romans 8:31)
4:18 There is no fear in perfect love.
4:20 If you say you love God but hate your brother, you are a liar.
5:3 God's commandments are for your good and are not a burden.
5:13 It is important that you KNOW that you have eternal life.

Your Notes Here

Second John

1:11 Do not accept anyone who is teaching that Jesus is not God in the flesh.

Your Notes Here

Third John

We should assist those who are on a journey to do God's work. We should support them financially.

Your Notes Here

Jude (Judah)

Gloom and doom for those who deny Jesus is Christ the LORD. Examples given include places like Sodom and Gomorrah. (Deu. 29:23) Evil people.
On the other hand, Christians remain faithful and witness to those in darkness about the light of Jesus.

Your Notes Here

The Revelation

1:7 Jesus is coming back and everyone will see Him, including those who pierced Him.

1:9 God shows His love by correcting Christians.

1:20 This verse should have the words "call out" to replace "knock" because it is followed by "if anyone hear my voice." In many parts of the world it is very rude to knock. (Acts 10:18)

2 and 3 God identifies a fault with each of the seven churches. This calls for self-examination by churches and individuals. Do we have faults?

4:3 John saw a complete circle rainbow around the throne of God. This phenomenon can be seen from an airplane high in the sky.

5:1 A scroll with writing on both sides is like unto the Ten Commandments that were written on both sides.

(Exodus 32:15)

Scrolls on sheep skin were written on one side.

6:12 In the hymn "It Is Well With My Soul" we see the words, "sky rolled back like a scroll."

11:19 The Ark of the Covenant in heaven.

14: 13 If you are in Christ, death is fortunate.

15:2 If you look out the window of the church at the entrance to the cave where John penned The Revelation, you can see what he called a "sea of glass" as he was on the Island of Patmos.

16:19 The Great City (Jerusalem) split into three parts, as it is divided today between Christians, Jews and Muslims.

19:16 Is it a tattoo? Or symbolic?

21:6 Compare to the 'woman at the well' (John 4:10)

21:8 Here is a list of characteristics of those who will NOT be in heaven.

Your Notes Here

Appendices

Appendix One

Old Testament Books
Listed Alphabetically and Page Numbers

Appendix Two

Alphabetical Listing of New Testament Books and Page Numbers

Appendix Three

Raising the "Dead"

1 Kings 17:18 …no breath left in him. His soul was revived.

2 Kings 4: Elisha and the son of the Shulamite. He sneezed 7 times after mouth to mouth resuscitation.

2 Kings 13:20 Dead man was thrown on the bones of Elisha and came back to life. Got his breath back.

Luke 7:11-17 Son of widow funeral procession. Jesus said, "Young man I tell you, get up."

Luke 848-56 The daughter of the synagogue leader. The people said, "Your daughter is dead." But Jesus said, "She will be restored." Not brought back to life, but restored. In verse 52 Jesus made it clear. "She did not die, but is sleeping." Her spirit returned.

John 11:4 Lazarus "This sickness will not end in death." Jesus in verse 14 said, ' Lazarus is dead."

Acts 4:36 Dorcus, Peter prayed for her: "Tabitha, get up."

Acts 20:7 Eutychus was asleep and fell from the 3rd floor to hit the ground. Paul said, "Don't be upset, his life is in him."

Because a person says someone is dead does not mean he\she is medically dead. ONLY in the case of Lazarus does God say the person is dead. In which case, Jesus demonstrated that He is the resurrection and the life.

Appendix Four

Jesus the Stone Mason

Psalm 118:22 The stone which the builders refused is become the head stone of the corner. (Matt: 21:42 Jesus quoted Psalm 118: 22-23 referring to himself.)

Isaiah 8:14 And he shall be for a sanctuary; but for a stone of stumbling and for a rock of offence to both houses of Israel, for a gin and for a snare to the inhabitants of Jerusalem.

 26:16 Therefore, thus saith the LORD GOD, Behold, I lay in Zion for a foundation

 a stone, a tried stone, a precious corner stone, a sure foundation: he that believeth shall not make haste.

Daniel 2:34 Thou sawest till that a stone was cut out without hands, which smote the image upon his feet that were of iron and clay, and brake them to pieces. :35…and the stone that smote the image became a great mountain and filled the whole earth. :45 Forasmuch as thou sawest that the stone was cut…

Zechariah 3:9 For behold the stone that I have laid before Joshua;

:7…and he shall bring forth the headstone thereof with shoutings, crying, Grace, grace unto it.

10:4 Out of him came forth the corner (Matt: 21:42; 1 Peter 2:6 corner stone)

Matt: 21:42 Jesus saith unto them, "Did ye never read in the scriptures, The stone which the builders rejected, the same is become the head of the corner?"

Mark 13:2 And Jesus answering said unto him, Seest thou these great buildings? There shall not be left one stone upon another that shall not be thrown down.

1 Peter 2:4 To whom coming, as unto a living stone, disallowed indeed of men but chosen of God and precious. :7-8 Unto you therefore which believe he is precious: but unto them which be disobedient, the stone which the builders disallowed, the same is made the head of the corner, and a stone of stumbling, and a rock of offence, even to them which stumble at the word, being disobedient:

Luke 20:17-18 And he beheld them, and said, What is this then that is written, The stone which the builders rejected, the same is become the head of the corner? Whosoever shall fall upon that stone shall be broken; but on whomsoever it shall fall, it will grind him to powder.

Acts 4:11 This is the stone which was set at nought of you builders, which is become he head of the corner.

If you visit Nazareth you can see the quarry where Joseph and Jesus worked. The site is preserved. The only direct reference to Jesus and wood was when he carried the cross.

Appendix Five

Tracing Jesus from Genesis To Revelation

In Genesis: He is the Seed of the Woman

In Exodus: The Passover Lamb

In Leviticus: The Perfect Sacrifice

In Numbers: The Lifted Up One

In Deuteronomy: The Prophet Like Moses

In Joshua: The Captain of Our Salvation

In Judges: The Deliverer

In Ruth: The Kinsman Redeemer

In 1 & 2 Samuel: The Prophet of the LORD

In 1 & 2 Kings, 1 & 2 Chronicles: The Reigning King

In Ezra: The Faithful Scribe

In Nehemiah: The Rebuilder of Broken Walls

In Esther: The Advocate

In Job: The Ever-living Redeemer

In Psalms: The LORD Who is our Shepherd

In Proverbs and Ecclesiastes: Wisdom and Purpose

In Song of Solomon: The Lover of Our Soul

In Isaiah: The Suffering Servant

In Jeremiah and Lamentations: The Weeping Prophet

In Ezekiel: The Glory of God

In Daniel: The Fourth Man in the Fiery Furnace

In Hosea: The Forgiving Bridegroom

In Joel: The Giver of the Holy Spirit

In Amos: The Burden Bearer

In Obadiah: The Mighty Savior

In Jonah: The Forgiving God

In Micah: The Ruler of all Ages

In Nahum: The Avenger of God's Elect

In Habakkuk: The Great Evangelist

In Zephaniah: The Restorer of God's Lost Heritage

In Malachi: The Sun of Righteousness, with Healing in His wings.

In Matthew: The Jewish Messiah

In Mark: The Servant

In Luke: The Son of Man

In John: The Son of God

In Acts: The Giver of the Holy Spirit

In Romans: The Justifier of Sinners

In 1 & 2 Corinthians: The Definition of Love

In Galatians: The One Who Sets Us Free

In Ephesians: The Exalted One

In Philippians: Our Great Joy

In Colossians: The Fullness of the Godhead

In 1 & 2 Thessalonians: The Soon Coming King

In 1 & 2 Timothy: The Mediator Between God and Man

In Titus: The Faithful Pastor

In Philemon: Our Covenant Friend

In Hebrews: The Messenger of the New Covenant

In James: The Great Physician

In 1 & 2 Peter: The Cornerstone

In 1& 2 & 3 John: Everlasting Love

In Jude: The One Who is Able to Keep Us

In Revelation: The King of Kings and LORD of LORDs!

  The Alpha and Omega

  The Beginning and the End